"Walter Brueggemann has done a great s[ervice to the Jew]ish people and to all who rely on the [Hebrew Bible as a] guide to life by demonstrating in this book that there is no straight line between these ancient holy texts and the oppression of the Palestinian people by an expansionist Zionist government in modern Israel. Christian Zionists are not serving the interests of the Jewish people or being loyal to God when they champion oppressive policies that violate the most frequent command in the Torah, namely variations on the Torah's command to 'love the stranger/ the Other,' to extend generosity toward them, and to be sure that they are given equal treatment before the law. Brueggemann's carefully reasoned reading of the Bible should become a stumbling block to those who give blind support to the policies of the state of Israel toward Palestinians, policies that are destructive not only to the Palestinians but also to Israelis, setting them on a course that in the long run will be destructive not only to those Jews who live there but also to Jews around the world who are increasingly being seen through the lens of Israel's arrogant policies toward their neighbors whom they have been commanded to love by the Torah. For those Jews who have turned away from Judaism because they see it increasingly becoming an idolatrous worship of Jewish nationalism, Brueggemann's book will be an important warning: don't abandon Judaism by allowing militarist readings of its texts to turn you away from the love-oriented tradition deep in Judaism that was embraced by the prophets, by Jesus, and by the early Christians."

—Rabbi Michael Lerner, editor of *Tikkun*, a Jewish magazine; chair of the Network of Spiritual Progressives; and author of *Jewish Renewal: A Path to Healing and Transformation* and *Embracing Israel/Palestine: A Strategy for Middle East Peace*

"Walter Brueggemann has trained his hermeneutic skills, keen perception of history, and deep faith on one of the most important human rights issues confronting the church and the world at large today. Brueggemann's greatness lies in his willingness, indeed his drivenness, to challenge accepted ways of looking at things—always searching, always open to the new, inviting us, as he concludes in this book, to 'differentiate between old mantras and urgent truthfulness.' Brueggemann shines a bright light on the core issues—justice, decency, and faithfulness to the tradition in which he is so deeply rooted.

This is a groundbreaking and terribly important book, because of the authority Brueggemann brings and because theological investigation is the key that will free Palestinians as well as Israelis from the current tragic impasse. 'How do we read the Bible?' Brueggmann asks. 'Is it credible to make any direct appeal from the ancient promises of land to the state of Israel?' We must, he declares, 'have the courage to deal with the political realities without being cowed by accusations of anti-Semitism.' The 'exclusion of the other is a suicidal policy' Brueggemann continues, asking those who support modern Israel's territorial claims to be 'suspicious of any reading of the Bible that excludes the other' and challenging us to engage with him in bringing the ancient texts into a dialogue with history and with our present circumstances. We expect no less from Walter Brueggemann. As ever, Brueggemann's voice, his compassion, and his courage are a beacon, shining a light where it most needs to be shone."

—Mark Braverman, Executive Director of Kairos USA
and author of *Fatal Embrace: Christians, Jews, and the Search for Peace in the Holy Land*

"Can the church discuss volatile issues? And among those topics, few are as volatile as the conflict between Israel and Palestine. In this small book, Walter Brueggemann serves as courageous prophet and irenic guide, providing us with summary positions on the Scriptures, their application to modern Israel, and careful questions for group discussion. This may be the best guide yet to help the church talk about a matter of enormous importance for our generation."

—Gary M. Burge, Professor of New Testament, Wheaton College and Graduate School; and author of *Jesus and the Land: The New Testament Challenge to Holy Land Theology*

"For too long Christians were connecting biblical Israel with the state of Israel. For too long the human rights of the Palestinians were violated in the name of divine rights. For too long theological naiveté about the chosen people had led to rejecting my own people, the Palestinians. I'm glad to see Dr. Brueggemann altering his own view. I commend this book to all those struggling with these questions and all who are concerned for peace and justice in the land called Holy."

—Dr. Mitri Raheb, President of Diyar Consortium and Dar al-Kalima University College in Bethlehem; President of the Synod of the Evangelical Lutheran Church in Jordan and the Holy Land; Senior Pastor of the Evangelical Lutheran Christmas Church in Bethlehem, Palestine; and author of sixteen books, including *Faith in the Face of Empire: The Bible through Palestinian Eyes*

"Brueggemann offers an honest critique of a belief system that reduces faith to a self-serving ideology and warns against a Christian reading of the Bible that reduces it to an ideological prop for the state of Israel."

—Rev. Dr. Naim Stifan Atee, a Palestinian priest in the Anglican Church, founder of the Sabeel Ecumenical Liberation Theology Center in Jerusalem, and an active leader in the shaping of the Palestinian liberation theology

"While the majority of our politicians, religious journals, and elected officials have been silent about the injustices that plague the 'un-holy land,' Walter Brueggemann has admittedly rethought these issues and provides here a theologically courageous and prophetic volume that is sure to assist our personal and collective journeys on 'the things that make for peace.' Readers will find profound hermeneutical insights on such vital issues as political and religious Zionism, the land, ancient Israel vs. modern Israel, supercessionism, 'chosen' people, and exceptionalism. This important volume could be a 'game changer' for pastors, congregational study, denominational policy, the academy, religious journals, and hopefully elected officials who continue to fail the Palestinians, Israelis, and their own constituents with decades of misguided Middle East policies."

"Brueggemann says what many who care deeply about the Middle East are thinking. Yes, ancient 'Israel is God's chosen people. That conviction is not in doubt in the Bible.' But given the current massive military buildup, the growing occupation of Palestinian land, and Israel's massive indifference to the human rights of Palestinians, 'Israel cannot expect to get much "positive play" from its identity as "God's chosen people."' Brueggemann reminds all that the Bible says 'the land is held *conditionally,* depending on obedience to the Torah' i.e. that 'the land is given unconditionally but it is held conditionally.'

In facing these competing assertions of chosenness and chosenness with conditions, Walter Brueggemann has attempted to penetrate the 'gridlock' within both the Christian and the Jewish community with respect to the nature, existence, and future of Israel and of their Palestinian neighbors. He does so by juxtaposing the exclusionist or 'purity' traditions developed during the Babylonian deportation under the leadership of Ezra, with the more welcoming, open traditions found in the Deuteronomic tradition. Both are biblical. It is an evenhanded effort to enable a fresh conversation among all of us who share his unequivocal commitment to the strength and security of Israel with an equal commitment to a viable, secure future for the Palestinian community."

"Indeed God cares to see that everybody lives with dignity and security and in a home. The promised land is indeed a land of promise, where God is honored and freely worshiped, justice is followed, and God is pleased to dwell in. I thank God for courageous scholars like Dr. Brueggemann who read the Bible in the light of the Truth of God."

—Dr. Mary Mikhael, past President and Professor of Christian Education, Near East School of Theology in Beirut, Lebanon; and author of the popular 2010 Horizons Bible study *Joshua: A Journey of Faith*

"At its essence, this book is about inclusion. No matter what you think about who God's chosen people are, Professor Brueggemann is clear and starkly honest in his assessment of the untenable nature of the modern state of Israel's treatment of the Palestinians. Methodically, he suggests an inclusive approach to reading the biblical texts that embraces the other. Such an exegesis is especially necessary today. This book is a welcome refocusing of a faith lens that has been too often used in the past—especially in the context of the Israelis and Palestinians—to exclude and appropriate rather than include and edify."

—Dr. Peter Makari, Executive for the Middle East and Europe, Global Ministries of the United Church of Christ and Christian Church (Disciples of Christ); and author of *Conflict and Cooperation: Christian-Muslim Relations in Contemporary Egypt*

"This book is written for Christians and Jews who take seriously God's promises to Israel in the Hebrew Scripture but who are troubled by how contemporary Palestinians are being treated by modern Israelis. Walter Brueggemann engages the actual words of the Bible and, in so doing, affirms the continued validity of God's promise to Israel and critiques as simplistic and anachronistic any interpretation of the Bible that presupposes a one-to-one correlation between the promises to biblical Israel and the political goals of the present Israeli government or the land acquisition plans of present-day settlers.

This book will deepen the theology of Christians and Jews who can't see any connection between the biblical land of promise and the current land of Israel; it will stretch the thinking of Christian and Jewish Zionists who overlook the key themes of justice and welcoming strangers in the biblical text; and it will deepen the biblical understanding of all who read it. It is simply the best book on its subject that I have read."

—Dr. Duncan Hanson, area supervisor for the Middle East, Europe, and India for the Reformed Church in America

CHOSEN?

Also by Walter Brueggemann
from Westminster John Knox Press

Abiding Astonishment: Psalms, Modernity, and the Making of History
(Literary Currents in Biblical Interpretation series)
Cadences of Hope: Preaching among Exiles
The Collected Sermons of Walter Brueggemann, Volumes 1 and 2
First and Second Samuel (Interpretation series)
From Whom No Secrets Are Hid: Introducing the Psalms
Genesis (Interpretation series)
Great Prayers of the Old Testament
Hope for the World: Mission in a Global Context
Hope within History
An Introduction to the Old Testament: The Canon and Christian Imagination, Second Edition (with Tod A. Linafelt)
Isaiah 1–39 (Westminster Bible Companion series)
Isaiah 40–66 (Westminster Bible Companion series)
Journey to the Common Good
Living Countertestimony: Conversations with Walter Brueggemann (with Carolyn J. Sharp)
Mandate to Difference: An Invitation to the Contemporary Church
Many Voices, One God: Being Faithful in a Pluralistic World (with George W. Stroup)
Power, Providence, and Personality: Biblical Insight into Life and Ministry
Reverberations of Faith: A Theological Handbook of Old Testament Themes
Sabbath as Resistance: Saying No to the Culture of Now
Struggling with Scripture (with Brian K. Blount and William C. Placher)
Texts for Preaching: A Lectionary Commentary (with Charles B. Cousar, Beverly Roberts Gaventa, J. Clinton McCann, and James D. Newsome)
Truth Speaks to Power: The Countercultural Nature of Scripture
Using God's Resources Wisely: Isaiah and Urban Possibility
The Vitality of Old Testament Traditions, Second Edition (with Hans Walter Wolff)

CHOSEN?

Reading the Bible amid the Israeli-Palestinian Conflict

WALTER BRUEGGEMANN

WESTMINSTER
JOHN KNOX PRESS
LOUISVILLE · KENTUCKY

First edition
Published by Westminster John Knox Press
Louisville, Kentucky

15 16 17 18 19 20 21 22 23 24—10 9 8 7 6 5 4 3 2 1

Book design by Erika Lundbom
Cover design by designpointinc.com
Cover photos: Flag of Palestine on brick wall ©iStock.com / creisinger;
Aged paper ©iStock.com / iSailorr;
Flag of Israel on brick wall ©iStock.com / creisinger

Library of Congress Cataloging-in-Publication Data
Brueggemann, Walter.
  Chosen? : reading the Bible amid the Israeli-Palestinian conflict / Walter Brueggemann. -- First edition.
     pages cm
  ISBN 978-0-664-26154-2 (alk. paper)
  1. Bible--Criticism, interpretation, etc. 2. Bible--Textbooks. 3. Arab-Israeli conflict--Religious aspects--Christianity. I. Title.
  BS511.3.B78 2015
  221.6--dc23

                                                                    2015002760

Most Westminster John Knox Press books are available at special quantity discounts when purchased in bulk by corporations, organizations, and special-interest groups. For more information, please e-mail SpecialSales@ wjkbooks.com.

For
Joe Phelps
my intrepid, faithful friend

CONTENTS

ACKNOWLEDGMENTS

THE CONFLICT BETWEEN ISRAEL AND THE PALESTINIAN people is not a static issue that permits frozen convictions unresponsive to the changing texture of the conflict. Most unhelpful, so it seems to me, is the temptation to hold to old political convictions that are not reconsidered in light of dramatically new circumstances. Because the issues change over time, it is essential that responsible thought and responsible policy should change as well. My own convictions concerning this conflict, as those of many other people, have changed considerably over time, a change that I judge responsible in the face of changing political reality.

Mindful of the long history of Christian anti-Semitism and the deep fissure of the Shoah, we have surely been right to give thanks for the founding of the state of Israel and the securing of a Jewish homeland. But the issues have altered dramatically as the state of Israel has developed into a major military power that continues administrative-military control of the Palestinian territories.

My own study of the conflict, reflected in these pages, has been informed by the witness of Naim Stifan Ateek and the ongoing work of Sabeel. Sabeel is a grassroots movement in East Jerusalem by Palestinian Christians working for a just peace in Palestine and Israel. In his book *Palestine: Peace not Apartheid*, Jimmy Carter issued a dramatic wake-up call that summoned readers to a fresh consideration of practices and policies that claim to be grounded in the promissory traditions of the Hebrew Bible. Most important for me has been an ongoing conversation with Mark Braverman, who by his rethinking the issue has invited many others to rethink it as well. Braverman, moreover, has introduced me to the important testimony of Israeli peace advocates who have the courage to think beyond slogans. I am, in addition, a fellow traveler with the Presbyterian Church (U.S.A.) in its continuing travail over divestment in Israel. As I have become aware of the depth and complexity of these issues, in what follows I offer my attempt to fulfill my vocation as a teacher of the church. The matters discussed here are endlessly contested and will continue to be so; if they were not, we would not be struggling with them so. Such contestation, however, does not relieve us of the obligation to bear witness as we are able. I am grateful to David Maxwell for suggesting this piece and seeing to its publication. I am, as always, grateful to WJK editors who turn words into books.

I am glad to dedicate this effort to my friend Joe Phelps, an intrepid minister of the gospel who remains steadfast and courageous on a variety of urgent issues that concern the church. He and I have not spent time together on the Israeli-Palestinian conflict, and he is not responsible for my views here. But his courage has been an important ingredient for my rethinking, and I am grateful to him.

Walter Brueggemann
Columbia Theological Seminary
Advent 2014

INTRODUCTION

THE SEEMINGLY INSOLVABLE CONFLICT BETWEEN THE STATE of Israel and the Palestinian people requires our best thinking, our steadfast courage, and a deep honesty about the politically possible. The conflict is only "seemingly" beyond solution, because all historical-political problems have solutions if there is enough courage, honesty, and steadfastness.

The conflict is not a fixed, unchanging situation; rather, it is a dynamic historical reality that is dramatically changing and being redefined over time. As a result, it is imperative that our thinking not be settled in a fixed position but that it be regularly reevaluated in response to the changed and changing realities on the ground. If we should settle for a fixed solution, then we will have arrived at an ideology, which is quite unhelpful for real problems on the ground.

In my own thinking, which is much influenced by my work as a Scripture scholar, I begin with a focus on the claim of Israel as God's chosen people. That conviction is not in doubt in the Bible. It is a theological claim, moreover, that fits with compelling persuasiveness with the reality of Jews in the wake of World War II and the Shoah. Jews were indeed a vulnerable people whose requirement of a homeland was an overriding urgency. Like many Christians, progressive and evangelical, I was grateful (and continue to be so) for the founding and prospering of the state of Israel as an embodiment of God's chosen people. That much is expressed in my earlier book entitled *The Land*. I took "the holy land" to be the appropriate place for the chosen people of the Bible which anticipates the well-being of Israel that takes land and people together.

Of course, much has changed since then in the linkage between the state of Israel and the destiny of the chosen people of God.

– The state of Israel has evolved into an immense military power, presumably with a nuclear capacity. There is no doubt that such an insistence on military power has been in part evoked by a hostile environment in which the state of Israel lives, including periodic attacks by neighboring states.

– The state of Israel has escalated (and continues to escalate) its occupation of the West Bank by an aggressive development of new settlements.

– The state of Israel has exhibited a massive indifference to the human rights of Palestinians.

Thus, it seems to me that the state of Israel, in its present inclination and strategy, cannot expect much "positive play" from its identity as "God's chosen people."As a consequence, my own judgment is that important initiatives must be taken to secure the human rights of Palestinians. This changed stance on my part is reflected in the new edition of my book on the land. It is a change, moreover, that is featured in the thinking of many critics who have been and continue to be fully committed to the security of the state of Israel, as am I.

This rethinking is important both for political reasons and for more fundamental interpretive issues. A change in attitude and policy is important to help resolve the conflict. It is clear enough that the state of Israel will continue to show little restraint in its actions toward Palestinians as long as U.S. policy gives it a "blank check" along with commensurate financial backing. Such one-sided and unconditional support for the state of Israel is not finally in the interest of any party, for peace will come only with the legitimation of the political reality of both Israelis and Palestinians. As long as this issue remains unaddressed, destabilization will continue to be a threat to the larger region.

It will not do for Christian readers of the Bible to reduce the Bible to an ideological prop for the state of Israel, as though support for Israel were a final outcome of biblical testimony. The dynamism of the Bible, with its complex interactions of the chosen people and other peoples, is fully attested, and we do well to see what is going on in the Bible itself that is complex and cannot be reduced to a simplistic defense of chosenness. The Bible itself knows better than that!

It is my hope that the Christian community in the United States will cease to appeal to the Bible as a direct support for the state of Israel and will have the courage to deal with the political realities without being cowed by accusations of anti-Semitism. It is my further hope that U.S. Christians will become more vigorous advocates for human rights and will urge the U.S. government to back away from a one-dimensional ideology for the sake of political realism. It seems to many of us that the so-called two-state solution is a dead possibility, as Israel in its present stance will never permit a viable Palestinian state. We are required to do fresh thinking about human rights in the face of the capacity for power coupled with indifference and cynicism in the policies of the state of Israel, which is regularly immune to any concern for human rights.

I have not changed my mind an iota about the status of Israel as God's chosen people or about urgency for the security and well-being of the state of Israel. Certainly the Christian West continues to have much to answer for with its history of anti-Semitic attitudes and policies. None of that legacy, however, ought to cause blindness or indifference to political reality and the way in which uncriticized ideology does enormous damage to prospects for peace and for the hopes and historical possibilities of the vulnerable. The attempt to frame the Israeli-Palestinian conflict in terms of anti-Semitism is unpersuasive. More courage and honesty are required amid the realities of human domination and human suffering. As the hymn writer James Russell Lowell wrote in reference to the U.S. Civil War, "New occasions teach new duties." The current conflict, with its escalation of cynical violence, is a new occasion. New duties are now required.

Chapter 1

READING THE BIBLE AMID THE ISRAELI-PALESTINIAN CONFLICT

THE ONGOING CONFLICT BETWEEN THE STATE OF ISRAEL and the Palestinian people is intense and complex, and it offers no easy or obvious solution. This chapter considers how to read the Bible responsibly in the midst of that conflict and consider what, if any, guidance may be received from it.

Reading the Bible with reference to any contemporary issue is at best tricky and hazardous, and any conclusion drawn from it is not likely to be persuasive to all parties in the dispute. People of faith can read the Bible so that almost any perspective on a current issue will find some support in the Bible. That rich and multivoiced offering in the Bible is what makes appeals to it so tempting—and yet so tricky and hazardous, because much of our reading of the Bible turns out to be an echo of what we thought anyway.

THE ISSUE OF LAND

The dispute between Palestinians and Israelis is elementally about land and secondarily about security and human rights. Various appeals are made to the Bible, especially concerning the disputed land. The appeal of the contemporary state of Israel to the Bible concerning the land is direct and simple. It is that the land of promise was given initially and unconditionally to Israel and thus to the ongoing community of Jews. It is a promise made to Abraham, reiterated to succeeding generations in the ancestral narratives of Genesis and then to the generation of the exodus.

A very different understanding of the land is offered in the covenant tradition of Deuteronomy and the prophets, wherein the land is held *conditionally*, depending upon obedience to the Torah. That tradition

---

Multiple Traditions in One Bible

Biblical scholars have identified a number of often competing traditions in the Hebrew Scriptures, or Old Testament. Not only were many books written by various authors, but many books also have multiple authors from multiple generations who edited previous writings. Part of the task of faithful interpretation is to acknowledge the variety of often competing positions found in the same Bible we say is the *Word of the Lord*.

in Deuteronomy, along with the prophetic tradition, asserts that the land is losable. It is possible to conclude that the land is given unconditionally but is held conditionally.

The reality of history is that the land was indeed losable, as the city of Jerusalem was destroyed in the sixth century BCE and the monarchal state of Judah under the Davidic dynasty lost its political identity. In the ongoing tradition after the deportation (exile) of the Jerusalem leaders, there was a great and inevitable interpretive dispute about the reasons why the land had been lost and the ways in which it might be returned and restored. Most likely, the great tradition of land promise and land reception was given final biblical form during this critical period. That final form of the promise took a long look back in history, but it was heavily influenced by the crisis of exile and sought to give legitimacy and assurance in the moment of restoration. The land promise as we have it is in some large part the accomplishment of fifth-century traditionists, an accomplishment that became the bedrock conviction for the Judaism that followed.

EZRA, THE EXCLUSIONIST

The reformulation of the tradition in the fifth century and the evocation of Judaism as heir to ancient Israel were accomplished under the leadership of Ezra the scribe. Ezra is remembered in Jewish tradition as second only to Moses as a religious leader. Ezra referred to the community as "the holy seed" (9:2). That phrase intends a biological identity, so Joseph Blenkinsopp can translate

Sorting Out Some Names and Dates

The term *Israel* came to be used in a variety of ways over the course of time. *Israelites* is the name given to all the descendants of Jacob, who was also called Israel (Gen. 35:10). Jacob, or Israel, had twelve sons, the ancestors of the twelve tribes of Israel. One of these sons was Judah. Things became confusing hundreds of years later when, two generations after King David's reign, the kingdom of Israel split into two nations. The northern kingdom continued to call itself Israel, and the southern kingdom took the name of its largest tribe, Judah.

After the northern kingdom was destroyed by Assyria in the eighth century BCE, *Israel* once again became available as a name for all the descendants of Jacob, including the Judeans. At this point, the names became somewhat interchangeable. Though the political name of the nation that was left remained *Judah* (and later *Judea*), and though the terms *Judaism*, *Jew*, and *Jewish* derive from this name, *Israel* continued to be used side by side with these terms.

Three other names are easier to distinguish. *Jerusalem* is the city in Judah that King David adopted as his capital. *Zion* is another name for Jerusalem. *Canaan* identifies the physical land that the Israelites occupied, because it was originally inhabited by Canaanites.

Key Dates	
1000 BCE	King David's reign
922 BCE	Israel divides into north (Israel) and south (Judah, which includes Jerusalem) after Solomon dies.
722 BCE	The Assyrians destroy and annex the north.
587 BCE	The Babylonians destroy the south and exile many leaders.
587–538 BCE	The Exile in Babylon (see glossary)
539 BCE	The Persians (now Iran) under King Cyrus conquer Babylon and then allow the exiles to return and rebuild the temple.

it as "holy race." Ezra's governance, moreover, led to the expulsion of foreign wives who had been acquired during the time of deportation (Ezra 9:1–4; Neh. 13:1–3, 23–30). The exclusion was in order to guarantee the purity of the land and of Israelite society.

BIBLICAL TENSION BETWEEN EXCLUSION AND WELCOME

The biological dimension of identity that necessarily concerned purity and the expulsion of outsiders created an ongoing ambiguity in Jewish identity, as noted by Blenkinsopp:

The factor of biological descent was certainly important and continues to be so, as is clear from the

> juridical definition of Jewish identity in the State of
> Israel today. What this means is that unlike Christian-
> ity, Judaism has continued to think of itself in terms
> of peoplehood. But it will be clear . . . that the pri-
> mary concern is with the *religious* identity of the com-
> munity, a concern which continues to be paramount
> throughout the Second Temple period[1]

That ambiguity about outsiders runs through Judaism,
as it does in Christian faith in a somewhat different
expression.

We should not, however, miss the emphasis on peo-
plehood that results, in one dimension of Judaism, as a
rather hard-nosed conviction about "one people in one
land" to the exclusion of others. Thus, the exclusion of
the foreign women becomes something of an epitome
or metaphor for the maintenance of purity that led as
well to the purity of the land, to the exclusion of all
others from the land.

Judaism also had and continues to have another
interpretive trajectory that makes welcome room for
the other. In the postexilic period, such an openness
is shown in the story of Jonah, wherein God shows
mercy toward Nineveh by sending Jonah to this perceived enemy of ancient Israel; in the narrative of Ruth,
which explains that David has a Moabite (non-Jewish)
mother, thus in violation of "the holy seed"; and in Isaiah 56, part of which concerns the welcome of foreign-
ers and eunuchs (two populations sure to jeopardize
purity) and includes God's promise "that my house
shall be called a house of prayer for all peoples" (v. 7).

In the current state of Israel with its Zionist policies, the exclusion of the other (now the Palestinians)

is a dominant motif. And while the state of Israel continues to "negotiate" with the Palestinians, the dominant Zionist appeal to land promises continues to hold intransigently to the exclusionary claim that all the land belongs to Israel and the unacceptable other must be excluded, either by law or by coercive violence.

The Bible is ambiguous about "the other." Some books and passages welcome the other; some reject the other. When this dialectic is brought to the matter of the land, it becomes an issue either of making room for the other in the land or of excluding the other from that land. Both parties can appeal to the Bible and find support for their interpretation.

MODERN TENSIONS: SAME OLD SAME OLD

The issue of Bible and land is whether to read with a welcome to the other or with an exclusion of the other. Welcome to the other appears to be a romantic dream in the world of real politics, and certainly current Israeli policy would find such openness to the Palestinians to be absurd. But if welcome to the other is considered romanticism, so ultimate exclusion of the other is a suicidal policy, because the other will not go away and cannot simply be wished away or forced away. As a result, the question of the other becomes the interpretive key to how to read the Bible. The other can be perceived, as in Zionist perspective, as a huge threat to the security of the state and the well-being of

> The question of the other becomes the
> interpretive key to how to read the Bible.
> . . . We ought rightly to be skeptical and
> suspicious of any reading of the Bible that
> excludes the other, because it is likely to
> be informed by vested interest, fears, and
> hopes that serve self-protection and end
> in suicidal self-destruction.

the holy seed. Conversely, the other can be perceived as a neighbor with whom to work at shalom.

The issue of exclusion or inclusion is one the Christian church also struggles with; the admission of Gentiles to the earliest Jewish Christian community occurred after a huge dispute and an enormous decision in which it finally came to be understood that the gospel concerns God's reach beyond settled boundaries to the other. That same interpretive dispute has been performed many times since in the ongoing world of faithful interpretation:

- Much of the Bible (in both Testaments) sanctions slavery. In Britain and the United States, ending slavery involved a hard interpretive struggle, and there exists a continuing legacy of racism.
- The patriarchal casting of the Bible treats women as second class. Only in recent times have women begun to be accepted as equal members of a welcoming community.
- Until recently, the Bible has been read as a judgmental text toward gays and lesbians as threaten-

ing others. Now that view has largely yielded to a welcome.

It is the same script being performed anew with every issue, and every time it is a difficult life-or-death issue. In the current Near East, the issue of the other is acute. It matters enormously how the Bible is read. The proponents of "holy seed" can readily appeal to the Bible, but the ongoing work of interpretation pushes us in a different direction. We know that how we read the Bible and where in the Bible we read is largely determined by our vested interest, our hopes, and elementally our fears—in many cases, our fear of the other. Martha Nussbaum has written concisely and eloquently about the issue in the wake of her study of the Hindu-Muslim conflict in India:

> The clash between proponents of ethnoreligious homogeneity and proponents of a more inclusive pluralistic type of citizenship is a clash between two types of people within a single society. At the same time, this clash expresses tendencies that are present, at some level, in most human beings: the tendency to seek domination as a form of self-protection, versus the ability to respect others who are different, and to see in difference a nation's richness rather than a threat to its purity.[2]

In response to the assumption that there is a "coming clash" between Western culture and Muslims, she concludes, "The real 'clash of civilizations' is not 'out there,' between admirable Westerners and Muslim zealots. It is here, within each person, as we oscillate uneasily between self-protective aggression and the ability to live in the world with others."[3]

Clearly, it is not simply exegesis that determines how we read the Bible; rather, it is our vested interests, our hopes, and our fears that largely determine our reading. And because the reach of the gracious God of the Bible is toward the other, we ought rightly to be skeptical and suspicious of any reading of the Bible that excludes the other, because it is likely to be informed by vested interest, fears, and hopes that serve self-protection and end in self-destruction. Palestinians' and Israelis' fear of the other, said to be grounded in the Bible, has been transposed into a military apparatus that is aimed at the elimination of the other. It is wholly illusionary to imagine that such an agenda is congruent with the God of the Bible who is commonly confessed by Jews and Christians.

SOME CONCLUSIONS ABOUT READING THE BIBLE

We may draw these conclusions about reading the Bible.

1. It is important in any case to recognize that the Bible refuses to speak in a single voice. It argues with itself, and we must avoid simplistic, reductionist readings of any ilk.

2. Any "straight-line" reading from ancient text to contemporary issues is sure to be suspect in its oversimplification. Such a reading disregards the huge impact of historical distance between the text and our current context.

3. Such a straight-line reading that ignores historical distance is most likely to be propelled by an ideology, that is, by a deeply held conviction that is immune to

critical thought and is unswayed by argument, by reason, or by the facts on the ground. That is, it disregards complexities in the process of interpretation. A one-dimensional, uncritical appropriation of the ancient land promises for the state of Israel is exactly such a conviction that is immune to critical thought, reason, or facts on the ground. The work of faithful interpretation and informed reading, however, is to attend to the complexities that relativize such convictions.

Responsible interpretation must pay attention to the disruptions that break open our long and deeply held preferences.

Just as one-dimensional Zionism is unrealistic in its oversimplification, so much Christian passion in support of Zionist ideology is also intellectually unreflective. This may take the form of a millennialist timetable that has been imposed on the biblical text. Or it may take the form of the romanticism of some liberals that compresses ancient Israel and the current state of Israel as though they were the same historical entity entitled to the same deference. Responsible interpretation must pay attention to the disruptions that break open our long and deeply held preferences.

4. The matter of ideological simplification versus responsible reading that pays attention to historical distance and interpretive complexity, when transposed into social power, becomes a contest between tribalism versus communitarian attentiveness to the other. Tribalism, often in Christian practice expressed as sectarianism, tends to absolutize its claims to the exclusion

of all else. The tribe or sect characteristically imagines that it has a final formulation, a final interpretation. Absolutist readings of the Bible lead to violent actions against one's opponent.

5. The other—as African slaves, or women, or gays and lesbians, or Palestinians—is not a disposable presence. It is, every time, a real and durable presence that will not go away. Proponents of the continuing racism in our society would like blacks to go away. Churches that resist women in leadership would like for women to go away. Much of society for a long time wanted gays and lesbians to go away. Hindus in India wish Muslims would go away. And surely Israeli Zionists want Palestinians to go away. Conversely many Arabs wish Israel would go away. But they will not. They cannot! And so room must be made. Making room for the other is a huge interruption of any absolutist claim.

6. In his elegant exposition of the Ten Commandments, Walter Harrelson has seen that the Decalogue, the core Torah requirement in Judaism, is a bottom line articulation of indispensible requirements of a viable society:

> The continuing witness of the Jewish people and of Jewish religious tradition is of great importance, for the Torah has the function of the Ten Commandments when the practice of dietary laws, Sabbath observances, and Jewish fidelity to Torah is not corrupted into a system of mere observances or mere regulations. . . . No, the central need is for people to know two fundamental things. The first thing people need to know is that they can have no real life, no real freedom, no real joy in life save as they lay aside the kinds of actions

that destroy the very things they are seeking. The Ten Commandments ward off conduct on our part which, if engaged in, will make impossible the love of God and of neighbor. The second is the need to know that we are being drawn toward the day appointed by God when people will indeed avoid these prohibitions, will love God and neighbor. We need to feel the lure, the drawing power of biblical eschatology.[4]

By the end of his exposition, Harrelson proposes that the Universal Declaration of Human Rights is an extension of the vision and creativity of the Decalogue. The Declaration includes these articles:

1. All human beings are born free and equal in dignity and rights.

2. Everyone has the right to life, liberty and the security of person.

7. All are equal before the law and are entitled without any discrimination to equal protection of the law.

15. Everyone has the right to a nationality.

17. No one shall be arbitrarily deprived of his property.[5]

These are all guarantees for the well-being of the other. The Israeli-Palestinian conflict cannot be resolved until the human rights of the other are recognized and guaranteed. These human rights are demanded by sociopolitical reality. They are, moreover, the bottom line of Judaism that has not been preempted by Zionist ideology. As Bishop Desmond Tutu has recently written:

Goodness prevails in the end. The pursuit of freedom for the people of Palestine from humiliation and persecution by the policies of Israel is a righteous cause. It is a cause that the people of Israel should support.

Nelson Mandela famously said that South Africans would not feel free until Palestinians were free.

He might have added that the liberation of Palestine will liberate Israel, too.[6]

Chapter 2

GOD'S CHOSEN PEOPLE: CLAIM AND PROBLEM

IN THE HEBREW BIBLE, ISRAEL IS PRESENTED AS GOD'S chosen people. It is a core declaration of the text and surely a continuing claim of Judaism. Indeed, the Bible makes no sense without this claim. The root of that theological claim can be found in at least three traditions in the Bible:

> In the *ancestral tradition of Abraham*, God enters into "an everlasting covenant" with the family of Abraham and promises "to be God to you and to your children after you" (Gen. 17:7). The drama of the book of Genesis, in each generation, is whether God will grant an heir who can carry the promise and live as God's covenant partner.

15

In the *exodus tradition*, God declares, "Israel is my firstborn son" (Exod. 4:22). In that ancient culture, that status as firstborn son is a role of special privilege and entitlement but also one of responsibility.

In the *Sinai tradition*, Israel is given opportunity to be God's "treasured possession out of all peoples" (Exod. 19:5).

In all of these traditions, the status of Israel is given by divine declaration that comes without explanation or grounding, the same kind of "arbitrariness" exhibited when God "had regard" for Abel and his offering to the neglect of Cain (Gen. 4:5). This divine decision is unilateral; it need not and cannot be explained. The several traditions make clear that from the earliest, Israel was given assurance and guarantee that is grounded in God's own initiative.

In these traditions, however, the specific language of "chosen" is not exactly used. It remained for Deuteronomy, which represents perhaps a later tradition, to utilize the most direct and unambiguous rhetoric for Israel's status as God's chosen people: "For you are a people holy to the Lord your God; the Lord your God has chosen you out of all the peoples on earth to be his people, his treasured possession" (Deut. 7:6).

The grounding of that status is not based on Israel as more "numerous" (Deut. 7:7) or more "righteous" (9:4, 6); rather, Israel is chosen because God "set his heart" on Israel and "loved" Israel (7:7–8; 10:15). There is nothing identifiable about Israel that would evoke such a decision and status. The rhetoric of "love" and "set one's heart" suggests that while the covenantal relation is formal and legal in character, there is a powerful emotive side to it. God is smitten with Israel!

That status, moreover, is reiterated and confirmed in exilic texts just at a time when one might conclude, in a context of displacement, that God had rejected Israel. The often repeated covenantal formula in exile confirms Israel's status as God's covenant partner: "I will be your God and you shall be my people" (Jer. 11:4; 24:7; 30:22; 31:33; Ezek. 11:20; 14:11; 36:18; 37:23, 27). The affirmation is against all of the historical evidence concerning Israel's exilic suffering, humiliation, and displacement.

IS THE CLAIM OF CHOSENNESS REVOCABLE?

It is possible to take this core claim at face value as a given theological fact that is straightforward and without problem. That, of course, is the intent of the Bible itself. Recently Joel Kaminski, a distinguished and reliable scholar, has taken it that way in his careful exposition of the theme (*Yet I Loved Jacob: Reclaiming the Biblical Concept of Election*). But many others have judged that the claim is difficult to accept and is deeply problematic. Two questions immediately present themselves: First, is that chosen status unconditionally given and therefore assured, or is it conditional and therefore revocable? This is an exceedingly difficult question, and the biblical texts seem to give more than one answer. It is a common assumption in the text that this status for Israel is unconditional. But in Exodus 19:5, at the outset of the Sinai tradition, there is a huge *if* in the invitation to covenant, suggesting that such status depends on attentive obedience to the Torah of Sinai without which Israel would forfeit that role. That *if* seems to be operative in much of the prophetic writings suggesting that Israel's status is in jeopardy. And indeed, in Isaiah 54:7–8 God concedes that "for a brief moment" God had abandoned Israel.

A second critical consideration is whether or to what extent that theological claim has come to be or has morphed into an ideological claim that functions as self-justification. Of course, the more the present state of Israel is drawn into the conversation, the more likely the question of ideology is likely to be raised. There is no reasonable or objective way to answer such a question, because every response has immense practical implications. That practicality concerns the distinction between and the overlap of the theological claims of Judaism and the political claims of the modern state of Israel. It would be splendid if we could consider the biblical text and its claims in and of themselves without reference to current practical matters, but in the present circumstance, that is not a realistic possibility. The question concerns the extent to which the claim is theological and so immune to such critical wonderment rather than being a claim that arises in and must make its way in the rough and tumble of Realpolitik. It is enough to see that the claim has been acutely problematized by the context in which we do theological reflection.

OTHER CONSIDERATIONS

We can identify three ways in which this ancient theme of chosenness has been otherwise appropriated. First, the notion of chosenness has been adapted in the Christian movement so that Jesus and the people around him (eventually the church) claim for themselves such a status. Such an appropriation of the theme amounts to a form of supersessionism—that is, that Christianity has superseded Judaism. This is so even when it is agreed that Jews and Christians may share the status as chosen. The notion that Christianity has displaced Judaism as the faith of the chosen is rooted in the idea that Judaism was a preparation for Christianity but that when Jesus came, Judaism no longer functioned. Such a belief is a historical absurdity and a theological scandal, but it has been a popular idea. The formulation of 1 Peter 2:9–10 is a close echo of Sinai and amounts to a claim for the church as the chosen of God. Indeed, in Galatians 6:16, Paul goes so far as to identify the community around Christ as "the Israel of God." He uses such phrasing to dismiss circumcision, thus challenging a decisive mark of chosenness by Jews that the

---

The notion that Christianity has displaced Judaism as the faith of the chosen is rooted in the idea that Judaism was a preparation for Christianity but when Jesus came, Judaism no longer functioned. Such a belief is a historical absurdity and a theological scandal, but it has been a popular idea.

---

tradition locates as early as Abraham (Gen. 17:10–14). Much Christian theology and even more hymnody have readily appropriated the claim of chosenness for the church. That claim made by the church derives from the claim made for Jesus as Messiah, so that the people after him are chosen after him.

Much Christian theology and even more hymnody have readily appropriated the claim of chosenness for the church.

Second, any consideration of the notion of chosen people must reckon with the way in which the phrase and the idea have been taken up in U.S. history as a way to understand and celebrate the United States. The claim of the chosenness of the United States, guaranteed by the providence of God, is very old in our national self-understanding. It is as old as the phrasing of "a city set on a hill" by the first governor among the Puritans.

Bruce Feiler *(America's Prophet: Moses and the American Story)* has traced the way in which public rhetoric in the United States has from the outset until now appealed to the role and leadership of Moses and has portrayed the United States as the emancipated people of God who came from Europe into the wilderness and found it to be the promised land. This includes Moses as the emancipator in the U.S. Civil War, as welcome to the stream of European immigrants in the late nineteenth century, and more recently in the rhetoric of Martin Luther King Jr. The notion of a promised land has figured strongly in U.S. rhetoric and self-understanding and has been a source of much hope for many immigrant communities. It has also had the pernicious spinoff of U.S. military expansionism under the claim that the "leader of the free world" must "save" benighted peoples in other lands. The national passion for expansionism, coupled with the missionary rhetoric of the church, has been infused with racism and a sense of national superiority. That notion of the United States as an exceptional nation, as the chosen of God, has caused a confused sense of state and church that is often evident in the zeal for an American flag in church sanctuaries, as though the linkage is essential and "natural" to a conviction of chosenness. Oddly enough, Russian president Vladimir Putin puckishly chided the United States for its assumed superiority as exceptional when he wrote this in the *New York Times:*

> I would rather disagree with a case he [Obama] made on American exceptionalism, stating that the United States' policy is "what makes America different. It's what makes us exceptional." It is extremely dangerous to encourage people to see themselves as exceptional, whatever the motivation. There are big countries and small countries, rich and poor, those with long democratic traditions and those still finding their way to democracy. Their policies differ, too. We are all different, but when we ask for the Lord's blessings, we must not forget that God created us equal.[7]

The influence of that exceptionalism is enormous, and it is no doubt appropriated from the chosenness of ancient Israel.

Third, in the last decades of the twentieth century, the Latin American Roman Catholic bishops settled on the formulation of "God's preferential option for the poor." This phrase asserts that the God of the gospel has a peculiar interest in and commitment to the poor, so that the poor become "the chosen" in this trajectory of interpretation. Jon Levenson, a noted Jewish interpreter, has protested against the notion of the poor as God's chosen people, as though to usurp the claim from the Jews to that status. The language of the bishops suggests that God has indeed taken sides with the poor against the rich and against the predatory practices and institutions of the rich.

Thus, we can identify these three claimants to the notion of chosenness, each of which has made a claim derivative from the Old Testament:

Christians as the newly chosen
Americans as the most recently chosen
The poor as the perennially chosen

Advocates of the several claims do not bother much to justify how these claims are made in the face of the unambiguous claim of the text for Israel. But that is in the nature of the claim; it is supple enough and readily appropriated and preempted for other people and communities.

WHAT ABOUT THE UNCHOSEN?

The matter of other peoples who are not chosen is a very important element in any talk about the chosen people. In the tradition of the ancestors in Genesis, there is clearly an awareness of the other peoples and an effort to make a place for them as those who are blessed by the life of Israel. The repeated formula "Nations shall be blessed" or "shall bless themselves" (Gen. 12:3; 18:18; 22:18; 26:4; 28:14) is belatedly taken up by Paul in his contention that the church must be open to Gentiles. Indeed, in Galatians 3:8 he takes the Abrahamic formula concerning the nations as "the gospel beforehand." That is, the good news concerns the reach of God's promise beyond Israel for the sake of other peoples. It is that admission of Gentiles—those who do not qualify under the Torah—as a part of God's people that is a distinguishing mark of the Christian movement as distinct from Judaism. One can, moreover, see at the edge of the Old Testament an inclusion of other peoples in the sphere of God's attentiveness, an inclusion that intends to mitigate any exclusionary claim by Israel. In Amos 9:7, in which the prophet intends to critique sharply the pride of Israel, he makes a claim that God enacts exoduses for other peoples as well as for Israel:

> Are you not like the Ethiopians to me,
> O people of Israel? says the Lord.
> Did I not bring Israel up from the land of Egypt,
> and the Philistines from Caphtor and the Arameans
>   from Kir?

In the later lines of this poem, the prophet names ancient Israel's two most immediate enemies, the Philistines and the Arameans, as recipients of God's deliverance. The text does not go so far as to name them as chosen of God, but the claim may be implied. Of course, it is this same Amos who says in his polemic against Israel

You only have I known [chosen] of all the families
    of the earth;
Therefore I will punish you for all your iniquities.

(3:2)

In this verse, the prophet acknowledges the singular chosenness of Israel, but it is that chosenness that evokes harsh divine judgment. The evident tension between Amos 9:7 and 3:2 indicates the edginess of the claim of chosenness, thus chosen for obedience but without monopoly of God's saving deeds, especially when presumed upon.

One can, moreover, see at the edge of the
Old Testament an inclusion of other peoples
in the sphere of God's attentiveness,
an inclusion that intends to mitigate any
exclusionary claim by Israel.

Even more daring is an oracle in Isaiah that imagines a time to come when other peoples, even the two great empires, will share in that status as the chosen: "On that day Israel will be the third with Egypt and Assyria, a blessing in the midst of the earth, whom the Lord of hosts has blessed, saying, 'Blessed be Egypt my people, and Assyria the work of my hands, and Israel my heritage'" (Isa. 19:24–25).

The three terms employed here are YHWH's pet names for Israel: "my people," "the work of my hands," "my heritage." God has now, according to the prophet, scattered these names across the world so that other peoples, even Israel's adversaries, are reckoned to be chosen of God. To be sure, such texts as Amos 9:7 and

Isaiah 19:24–25 are rare and likely too much should not be made of them. They do confirm, however, that Israel has an awareness that other peoples belong decisively in the purview of God's special favor, but the matter is never sorted out in the text, and Israel's claim for the most part remains unchallenged in the textual tradition.

CHOOSING BEYOND CHOSENNESS

Todd Gitlin and Liel Leibovitz have explored the claims for chosenness in contemporary Israel and the United States in their book *Chosen Peoples: America, Israel, and the Ordeals of Divine Election*. Their use of the term "ordeal" in their subtitle suggests that such an identity becomes a burden for the carrier. They say of these two claimants,

> Two nations, two histories, two cultures, two sets of assumptions march to the same drummer. At the heart of the special friendship between Israel and America lies an extraordinary spiritual-cum-ideological bond; their unshakable attachment to the wild idea of divine election, which, however dampened, however sublimated, continues to ripple beneath the surface of everyday events. . . . There is no rolling back the history that ensues. The clock cannot be reset to zero. We cannot choose to be unchosen. We cannot end the ordeal. The cycles of race hatred, revenge, and war cannot be rescinded, erased from memory. History is unsparing.[8]

They conclude with a riff on the unchosen, which in the present moment exactly pertains to the Muslims. The war against Muslims (who are treated as an

> It would seem that in every claim of chosenness—from Israel, the United States, the church—the chosen must choose beyond their chosenness.

undifferentiated mass) is a predictable counterpoint to chosenness. To cast some as chosen may evoke endless hostility toward others' lives at the brink of violence. It would seem that in every claim of chosenness—from Israel, the United States, the church—the chosen must choose beyond their chosenness. This is difficult, for it is against the grain of entitlement and assurance. But unless difficult choices are made, the present violence can only hold out a future of perpetual violence.

Chapter 3

HOLY LAND?

THE CURRENT CONFLICT BETWEEN THE STATE OF ISRAEL and the Palestinians raises the issue of land in the most contentious way. That complex issue has many dimensions, including political leverage, military capacity, and often unmentioned human rights abuses. It also includes deep memory and heritage. This latter dimension requires, among other things, that we consider the topic of land in the Old Testament. I believe that it is now impossible to consider the biblical theme apart from this contemporary dispute, even though the biblical legacy is only a small ingredient in the contemporary conflict.

THE GIFT

The theme of land (as in "holy land") permeates the ancient memory of Israel in the Old Testament. The

initial address of YHWH to Abraham concerns pre-
cisely land: "Now the Lord said to Abram, 'Go from
your country and your kindred and your father's house
to the land that I will show you'" (Gen. 12:1; see 15:18–
21). The promise is reiterated to Isaac: "To you and
your descendants I will give all these lands, and I will
fulfill the oath that I swore to your father Abraham. I
will make your offspring as numerous as the stars of
heaven, and will give to your offspring all these lands"
(Gen. 26:3–4). YHWH repeats the promise to Isaac's
son Jacob: "The land on which you lie I will give to you
and to your offspring" (Gen. 28:13).

The same promise is reiterated in the tradition of
Moses (Exod. 3:8). It is this promise that sets in motion
both the emancipation from Egypt and the onerous
journey through the wilderness on the way to the land
of promise. The land promised by God to Israel is given
without condition or obligation. It is a unilateral commitment on God's part.

GIFT WITH STRINGS ATTACHED

As the tradition unfolds, however, two matters come to
hand. First, in the extended speeches of Moses in the
book of Deuteronomy, Moses sets forth a set of commandments and ordinances that must be kept if the
land of promise is to be retained. Moses warns Israel
against the temptation to self-sufficiency that leads to
disobedience and thus to land forfeiture: "Do what is
right and good in the sight of the Lord, so that it may
go well with you, and so that you may go in and occupy
the good land that the Lord swore to your ancestors to
give you (Deut. 6:18; see 8:17–19; 11:22–25).

The capstone of this conditional *if* is the long recital of blessings and curses in Deuteronomy 28, in which obedience to Torah becomes a prerequisite for holding the land. It is clear that this Deuteronomic *if* challenges the unconditional promise to the ancestors. Thus, we may conclude that the land is *given* to Israel unconditionally, but it is *held* by Israel conditionally. We may also conclude that this unmistakable tension in the tradition ensures that different advocates will be drawn to different texts, as the textual tradition itself yields no single verdict.

Thus, we may conclude that the land is *given* to Israel unconditionally, but it is *held* by Israel conditionally.

The Deuteronomic *if* became a primary theme among the prophets of the eighth and seventh centuries BCE. In their various speeches of judgment, the prophets voice indictment of Israel for violation of Torah—a failure to practice justice and holiness—and they conclude that the land of promise will only be held if the Torah is honored.

THE TORAH ONLY ANTICIPATES LAND

The second matter has to do with the fact that the five books of the Torah, the most authoritative textual tradition in the Hebrew Bible, ends before Israel enters the land (see Deut. 34:4). That is, Israel's original or earliest tradition is not about having the land; it is about anticipating the land. At that point of anticipation, the Torah ends, as does the life of Moses.

The reason this particular ending to the Torah is important is that critical judgment now has concluded that the Torah was formulated in the fifth century during the Persian period. The tradition surely has old stories and themes in it, but the compilation of writings that became Scripture was accomplished in the Persian period among the elite community of Jews who had been deported (exiled) by the Babylonians.

This means that we are required to read the tradition with a double vision. On the one hand, we read it

---

The Exile

In July 587 BCE, Babylonian soldiers broke through Jerusalem's walls, ending a starvation siege that had lasted well over a year. They burned the city, and Solomon's temple and took its king and many other leaders to Babylon as captives, leaving others to fend for themselves in the destroyed land. Many surrounding countries disappeared altogether when similar disasters befell them. But Judah did not. Instead, the period scholars most often call the "Babylonian exile" inspired religious leaders to revise parts of Scripture that had been passed down to them. It also sparked the writing of entirely new Scriptures and the revision of ideas about God, creation, and history. Much of what is called the Hebrew Scriptures or Old Testament was written, edited, and compiled during and after this national tragedy.

as presented, as an ancient account of promise and wilderness sojourn. On the other hand, we read it through
the lens of Persian-period displaced Jews who longed
for a return to the long lost land of Judah. These vigorous hopers would have understood the wilderness
tradition found in the book of Numbers as their own
contemporary experience of displacement. Thus, the
account in Deuteronomy of the arrival at the Jordan
River, the boundary of the land of promise, was the
imagined arrival of the fifth-century displaced Jews
back into the land of promise. The old promises, now
greatly reformulated, became the ground of hope for
later generations of Jews.

Thus, when we "cross the Jordan" from the Torah
into the account of the land entry in Joshua 3–4, we
are in a very different world of land acquisition. Now
the land is not "promised" or "given"; it is taken by
force of arms. Thus, Joshua 12:7–24 can provide
an inventory of the "thirty-one kings" who were
defeated by Israel. That list, moreover, is supported
by earlier narratives of brutal fighting and victory
for Israel. The later story of land-taking, unlike the
Torah's story of land promise, pivots on the recognition that the land of promise was not empty. It was a
land fully and long occupied by those who had pre-
ceded Israel.

The several narratives of Joshua tell of a variety
of ways in which the arriving Israelites come to terms
with the resident population, terms that characteristically end with triumph for and control by the Israelites.
The summary statement of the book of Joshua links
the victory of Israel to the preceding land promises,

making clear that the actual victories were a "performance" of God's promises:

> Thus the Lord gave to Israel all the land that he swore to their ancestors that he would give them; and having taken possession of it, they settled there. And the Lord gave them rest on every side just as he had sworn to their ancestors; not one of all their enemies had withstood them, for the Lord had given all their enemies into their hands. Not one of all the good promises that the Lord had made to the house of Israel had failed; all came to pass. (Josh. 21:43–45)

God's promises were fulfilled, but only through the vigorous action of Israel. It is more than a little ironic (an exhibit of the same recurring tension) that this fulsome statement of promise fulfilled is promptly matched by a warning that reiterates the Deuteronomic *if*:

> If you transgress the covenant of the Lord your God, which he enjoined on you, and go and serve other gods and bow down to them, then the anger of the Lord will be kindled against you, and you shall perish quickly from the good land that he has given to you. (Josh. 23:16)

Thus, the land is *given*, the land is *taken*, and the land is *losable*.

It turned out that the narrative of the losability of the land, a view championed by the prophets, was correct. The land was lost! The city of Jerusalem was destroyed. According to Jeremiah's narrative report, "Judah went into exile out of the land" (52:27).

The small number of deportees in Jeremiah 52:8–10 suggests that many remained in the land; the elite opinion-makers were deported, however, and it is their story

that the Bible tells. The triumphant tone of Israel had
turned to grief as Israel sensed divine abandonment:

> But now you have spurned and rejected him [the king];
> you are full of wrath against your anointed.
> You have renounced the covenant with your servant;
> you have defiled his crown in the dust.
> You have broken through all his walls;
> you have laid his strongholds in ruins.
> ....
> Lord, where is your steadfast love of old,
> which by your faithfulness you swore to David?
> Remember, O Lord, how your servant is taunted;
> how I bear in my bosom the insults of the peoples,
> with which your enemies taunt, O Lord,
> with which they taunted the footsteps of your anointed.
>   (Ps. 89:38–40, 49–51)

Israel's grief could be even more vigorous:

> You have made us a byword among the nations,
> a laughingstock among the peoples.
> ....
> All this has come upon us,
> yet we have not forgotten you,
> or been false to your covenant.
> Our heart has not turned back,
> nor have our steps departed from your way.
>   (Ps. 44:14, 17–18)

The conditional *if* of the Torah has prevailed!

LAND RESTORED

In the dynamism of the tradition of Israel, however, a
remarkable thing happens. The story does not end with
land loss, displacement, and grief. Most stunningly, in
this season of deeply felt abandonment there wells up a

bold and vigorous reassertion of the land promise. The emergent prophetic voices insist in exile that the God who has abandoned Israel and caused forfeiture of the land is the God who will reperform the land promise. Thus, YHWH can both acknowledge abandonment and reassert restorative fidelity to Israel:

> For a brief moment I abandoned you,
> but with great compassion I will gather you.
> In overflowing wrath for a moment
> I hid my face from you,
> but with everlasting love I will have compassion on you,
> says the Lord, your Redeemer.
>
> (Isa. 54:7–8)

From this new wave of divine compassion comes expectation among the displaced for restoration in the land of promise, so that the reformulated "old tradition" now becomes a script to be performed again.

– Thus Jeremiah can anticipate restoration in the land (30:18; see the prose anticipation of 31:38–40);
– Ezekiel can delineate, in his characteristically precise way, the boundary lines of the recovered tribal legacies, boundary lines that have their counterpoint in the tradition of Joshua 13–19 (Ezek. 47:13–48:35);
– and, most of all, Isaiah in exile can imagine a glorious, triumphant procession of the exiles back home:

Depart, depart, go out from there!

For you shall not go out in haste,
and you shall not go out in flight;
for the Lord will go before you,
and the God of Israel will be your rear guard.
                    (52:11–12; see 55:12–13)

These lyrics of exilic hope for restoration are matched
in the historical narrative of 2 Chronicles 36:22–23,
the final verses of the Hebrew Bible. With this ending, the entire canon is claimed for and focused on
the homecoming and reentry into the land. Thus, the
land theme dominates the tradition and culminates in
hope, grounded in YHWH's resilient resolve of well-
being in the land that will be generative and fruitful
and secure.

HOW IMPORTANT IS THE LAND?

As we ponder the grand sweep of this vision that runs
from Abraham to King Cyrus of Persia, two questions
arise: First, how central and indispensible are the land
and the land promise for Judaism's existence? The contemporary Zionist movement would have us believe
that Judaism is equated with the land and, consequently, with support for the state of Israel as the present embodiment of the land of promise. Passion for
that understanding is greatly reinforced by the searing
memory of the Shoah (Holocaust), when Jews were
left without any safe place—that is, without a homeland. That equating of the *state of Israel* with the *faith
of Israel* draws heavily upon the biblical tradition. That
approach, however, amounts to a particular interpretive trajectory that is not required by the tradition, and

it disregards the Deuteronomic *if:* that the land is held conditionally. This interpretive position, like every interpretive position, requires a careful reading of carefully selected texts.

One compelling alternative to land theology is the recognition that Judaism consists most elementally in interpretation of and obedience to the Torah in its requirements of justice and holiness.

More crucial is the recognition that while the land tradition is of immense importance for the textual tradition, Judaism as it took form in the fifth century BCE was in fact not uniform and represented a variety of interpretive possibilities. Specifically, there were many Jews in exile who were not smitten with the land of Judah and who did not feel compelled by faith to return to the land.

One compelling alternative to land theology is the recognition that Judaism consists most elementally in interpretation of and obedience to the Torah in its requirements of justice and holiness. Such intense adherence to the Torah can be done anywhere at all. Thus, land theology is, at least in some traditions of Judaism, relativized by the recognition that Judaism is a "religion of the book" (the Torah) and consists in the practice and interpretation of texts. Robert Alter has noted that Judaism is primarily a "culture of interpretation" that refuses absolutizing any conclusions from the text; we may assume that this includes absolutizing conclusions about the land. The relativizing of the land promise permits the thought that the practice of Torah reaches beyond tribal or ethnic identity of a sectarian kind. Thus, Martin Buber, no friend of Zionism, can write of Abraham's promise of the land:

> This entire history of the road from Ur of the Chaldees to Sinai is a consequence of choices and partings, events of history—tribal history and national history. But above them stands revelation and gives them their meaning, points out to them their goal. For the end of all these partings is a true community of all men.[9]

The notion of "above them stands revelation" means that the Torah and the world it evokes are beyond a possessed land, and this notion links to "a true community of all" that transcends any tribalism.

IS TODAY'S ISRAEL BIBLICAL ISRAEL?

A second, closely related question concerns the direct appeal of the contemporary state of Israel to the land promise of the Bible in order to justify the geopolitical claims of Israel with particular reference to the scope of "Greater Israel," which includes the West Bank. Concerning any interpretive question, critical faith will resist a direct line from ancient text to contemporary claim.

The land issue is no exception to that general rule for critical interpretation. Consequently, it is simply not credible to make any direct appeal from the ancient promises of land to the state of Israel. That is so for two reasons. First, much has happened between text and contemporary political practice that resists such innocent simplicity. Second, because the state of Israel, perhaps of necessity, has opted to be a military power engaged in power politics along with the other nation-states of the world, it cannot at the same time appeal to an old faith tradition in a persuasive way. Thus, the state of Israel can, like any nation-state, make its legitimate political claims and insist upon legitimate security. But appeal to the ancient faith traditions about land promise in order to justify its claims carries little conviction except for those who innocently and uncritically accept the authority of that ancient story. At most, appeal to the land tradition can "energize the base," that is, evoke support from adherents to the ancient promise.

Such an appeal, however, carries little if any force for any who are outsiders to that narrative. It is no claim to be used in negotiations because it is grounded in theological claims to which Israel's adversaries will give no weight. The case for the state of Israel and its legitimate security is an important one. But it is a case that must be made, in my judgment, in terms of contemporary sociopolitical, military, and economic realities. The appeal to the biblical promise must simply be set alongside very old claims made by the Palestinians. Current Israeli leaders (seconded by the settlers) easily and readily appeal to the land tradition as though it were a justification for contemporary political ends. Nothing could be further from reality. Any and every appeal to ancient tradition must allow for immense interpretive slippage between ancient claim and contemporary appeal. To try to deny or collapse that space is illusionary. No one beyond one-dimensional ideologues (Israeli, Palestinian, or American) can work from such a claim. The textual tradition continues to sound its powerful claim, but it allows no final reading that would lead inevitably to a clear and lasting solution concerning vulnerable adversaries.

Chapter 4

ZIONISM AND ISRAEL

THE CITY OF JERUSALEM (ANCIENT JEBUS) WAS THE LAST territory of what became ancient "Israel" to be taken for Israelite possession and control (see Judg. 19:10–12). Even then, it became "the city of David"—thus, a personal possession of the king—not "the city of Israel." The capture of the city is reported in 2 Samuel 5:6–9 (see 1 Chron. 11:4–8); the city apparently was taken in a surprise attack by David's soldiers. The report highlights "the stronghold of Zion" on the southeastern hill of the city that became David's capitol and then the site of David's son Solomon's temple. That it was a fortification subsequently controlled by David is all that we know historically, though archaeological research has filled in many of the details.

ZION

The significance of the name *Zion* in the Old Testament, however, depends upon the poetic force of the term that transposed an actual place into the most sweeping liturgical claim. In poetic imagination, *Zion* came to refer to the larger symbolic significance of Jerusalem as the seat of the Davidic dynasty with its messianic implications, the site of Solomon's temple with its assurance of divine habitation (see 1 Kgs. 8:1), and the locus of Israel's most precious promises from God. In subsequent interpretive imagination, *Zion* became a reference point for all of the sociopolitical-theological claims of Jerusalem that came to dominate the hopes of Israel. It was, moreover, the center of an economy that supported a small urban elite who enjoyed surplus wealth resulting from peasant agriculture in the surrounding region. Eventually it became a summary for the city, with all of its political possibilities and its theological claims. The poetry does not distinguish between the city, the temple, the monarchy, and the political-military apparatus. Taken all together, they provide an image of well-being that is assured in the future that God will give to Israel.

In the hymnody of Israel (as in the book of Psalms), Zion is celebrated as a source of beauty and wonder:

His holy mountain, beautiful in elevation,
is the joy of all the earth.
Mount Zion, in the far north,
The city of the great King.
....
Walk about Zion, go all around it,

count its towers,
consider well its ramparts;
go through its citadels,
that you may tell the next generation
that this is God,
our God forever and ever.
He will be our guide forever.
                    (Ps. 48:1–2, 12–14)

It is the dwelling place of God:

In Judah God is known,
his name is great in Israel.
His abode has been established in Salem,
his dwelling place in Zion.
                    (Ps. 76:1–2)

It is a place imagined as a goal for pilgrimage:

Happy are those whose strength is in you,
in whose heart are the highways to Zion.
As they go through the valley of Baca
they make it a place of springs;
the early rain also covers it with pools.
They go from strength to strength;
the God of gods will be seen in Zion.
                    (Ps. 84:5–7)

While the name Zion is not used, the psalms that celebrate the wonders of Jerusalem (dubbed by commentators as "the Songs of Zion," on which see Psalm 137:3) show Jerusalem as a safe place fully protected by God. The best known of the Songs of Zion is Psalm 46, wherein the city itself vouches for the presence of God and the solidarity of God with Israel:

God is our refuge and strength,
a very present help in trouble.

....

God is in the midst of the city; it shall not be moved;
God will help it when morning dawns.

....

The Lord of hosts is with us;
The God of Jacob is our refuge.

(Ps. 46:1, 5, 7)

The best known of the Songs of Zion
is Psalm 46 wherein the city itself vouches
for the presence of God and the solidarity
of God with Israel.

Zion is a place for exaltation of YHWH over
the other gods in the temple liturgy (v. 10). It is the
venue where the kingship of YHWH is performed and
celebrated:

Zion hears and is glad,
and the towns of Judah rejoice,
because of your judgments, O God.
For you, O Lord, are most high over all the earth;
you are exalted far above all gods.

(Ps. 97:8–9)

Of course, the subsequent history of Jerusalem
placed in jeopardy these high claims for Zion when
the city was destroyed by the Babylonians in the sixth
century BCE. Many Jewish leaders were deported to
Babylon during this traumatic and pivotal time for
Israel. Thus, Zion is not only celebrated for its beauty
and splendor; it is also grieved in its loss. The lament
of Psalm 74 petitions God to remember Mount Zion,
which has been seemingly forgotten:

> Remember your congregation, which you acquired
>   long ago,
> which you redeemed to be the tribe of your heritage.
> Remember Mount Zion, where you came to dwell.
> Direct your steps to the perpetual ruins;
> the enemy has destroyed everything in the sanctuary.
> (Ps. 74:2–3)

The Psalm goes on to describe for God the shameful destruction of the temple:

> Your foes have roared within your holy place;
> they set up their emblems there.
> At the upper entrance they hacked
> the wooden trellis with axes.
> and then, with hatchets and hammers,
> they smashed all its carved work.
> (vv. 4–7)

The psalmist expects that when God is fully aware of the devastation, God not only will share in Israel's grief but will be moved to act to restore the splendor of the city:

> Rise up, O God, plead your cause;
> remember how the impious scoff at you all day long.
> Do not forget the clamor of your foes,
> the uproar of your adversaries that goes up continually.
> (vv. 22–23)

That same grief over Zion is voiced in the book of Lamentations (1:4, 6, 17; see 2:8).

In Psalm 137, voiced by exiled Jews in Babylon, grief over the destroyed city has turned to determination and resolve that has become the ground for intransigent hope:

By the rivers of Babylon—
there we sat down and there we wept
when we remembered Zion.

....

If I forget you, O Jerusalem,
let my right hand wither!
Let my tongue cling to the roof of my mouth,
if I do not remember you,
if I do not set Jerusalem
above my highest joy.

(Ps. 137:1, 5–6)

The memory of the destroyed city and the lost homeland leads to a cry for vengeance (vv. 7–9); but it also
voices hope for Jerusalem as "highest joy."

Three Isaiahs?

Scholars separate the book of Isaiah into three
sections. Chapters 1–39 are ascribed to the actual
prophet Isaiah, although future editors appear to
have reworked small parts of the material. He was
proclaiming his message to the south (Judah and
Jerusalem) from approximately 742 BCE until 722
BCE when the northern kingdom was destroyed
and then annexed to Assyria. The south survived
until the Babylonians destroyed it in 587 BCE.

Chapters 40–66 are commonly called Second
Isaiah (40–55) and Third Isaiah (56–66). They
originated immediately before the fall of Babylon
(539 BCE) to the Persians. Shortly after this time,
Jews living in Babylonian exile were permitted to
return and rebuild.

In the abundant faith of the sixth-century exiles, the remembered, destroyed city becomes a source of expectation for a restored Jerusalem. While God may have permitted the destruction of the city, God will not finally abandon the city, because God has a commitment to the city and its restoration that is as intransigent as the hope of the deportees. Thus, the Isaiah tradition can, in an anticipatory oracle, imagine a "surviving remnant" that will "take root downward and bear fruit upward" (Isa. 37:30–32; 2 Kgs. 19:29–31). In the poetry of Second Isaiah, the recovery and restoration of Zion is a primary theme:

> I bring near my deliverance, it is not far off,
> and my salvation will not tarry;
> I will put salvation in Zion,
> for Israel my glory.
> (46:13; see 51:3, 11, 16)

> Awake, awake,
> put on strength, O Zion!
> Put on your beautiful garments,
> O Jerusalem, the holy city.
> ....
> Loose the bonds from your neck,
> O captive daughter Zion!
> (52:1–2; see 60:14)

In Isaiah 62:1, God breaks the silence of exile and speaks words of promise and restoration that shatter the despair of Israel and break the grip of abusive empire. This poetry anticipates the economic recovery of the city (60:6–7, 11–12). From there, the prophetic tradition of ancient Israel is permeated with references to the coming well-being of Zion; this corpus of prophetic texts becomes the ground of hope among Jews for the recovery of Jerusalem and its surroundings. While this hope is not ever formulated as an "ism," it would be fair to say that the recurring pattern and frequency of this claim for the future of Jerusalem has become nearly an "ism"—that is, "Zionism"—with the conviction that God's commitment to and resolve for the ancient city of David and temple finally will prevail, thus ensuring safety and well-being for its restored population. These texts reveal Jerusalem's profound hope and expectation for a future Jerusalem, a "new Jerusalem" (imagined in some detail in Isa. 65:17–25).

There is no doubt that the Christian tradition has claimed for itself much of the imagery and phrasing that pertains to Zion, to Jerusalem, and to the king who reigns there. Thus, the new Jerusalem is an ultimate hope of the New Testament church (Rev. 21:2). That hope is expressed in the romantic Christmas carol "The Holy City." The church, moreover, has taken the Zion reference in such hymns as "O Zion, Haste" to mean the church in its missional practice. These usages, deeply rooted in Christian piety and hymnody, are part of the large legacy of Christian supersessionism whereby Christians have readily taken over Jewish forms and expressions of faith. Such usages are deeply problematic, but exploring that does not help us with the current issue concerning Zionism as it is expressed in the state of Israel.

MODERN ZIONISM

Modern Zionism arose in the nineteenth century as a Jewish movement conducted by determined advocates and persistent lobbyists so that Jews in the contemporary world would have a homeland. This Zionism made a compelling connection to the ancient biblical conviction concerning a restored, recovered Jerusalem. Unlike the Christian use of *Zion*, this "ism" refers to a real socioeconomic possibility about the restoration of the ancient land of Israel and the city of David as a contemporary possibility for Jews.

That advocacy and lobbying, which began as a small enterprise that received little attention, resulted in the formation of the state of Israel in 1948, a state that was presented as a full embodiment of the ancient promises of Zion. The story of the path from a small beginning to a legitimate state is a story of calculation, pressure, intrigue, passion, empathy, and a bit of happenstance. Midway in the movement toward a state, the turn of affairs in the midst of World War I was of immense importance. The Ottoman Empire, which had long presided over the territory that was to become the new state, ended at the hands of the British and French, who subsequently divided up its conquered territories. The British were keen to protect trade routes and began negotiations with the Jewish advocates while at the same time double-dealing with the Arabs about their own postwar expectations and demands.

A particular outcome of this complex and less-than-honest negotiation was the issuance of the Balfour Declaration in 1917. This policy statement from the British foreign secretary, Arthur Balfour, a Christian Zionist, committed Britain to a "homeland" for Jews. The Declaration did not use the term *state*, and no doubt British intentions were exceedingly vague amid the confusions and complexities of settling matters after the war. But the Declaration gave immense energy to the Jewish advocates for a homeland. In 1948, the declaration of the state of Israel quickly gained U.S. recognition, followed by UN recognition. The state of Israel could claim itself as the legitimate heir to the ancient promises of Zion.

At the outset, many matters between the state of Israel and the Palestinian population were unsettled and disputed, and the world powers that supported Israel, principally Britain and the United States, were fuzzy about them. But regional threats and actual resistance to the Jewish state resulted in the war of 1967 and the subsequent occupation of the West Bank by the state of Israel, which hardened positions on all sides. One outcome was a hardened Zionism that combined a desperate aspiration with an uncompromising ideology that supported the state of Israel and its security at all costs against all comers. As a result, the theological roots of the claim were skillfully allied with Israel's immense and growing military power and with the great degree of international empathy for Israel in the wake of the Shoah.

Like every ideology, Zionism hardened into a nonnegotiable cause that to many observers was no longer interested in or informed by the political facts on the ground. With its military capacity and the unflagging commitment of U.S. policy in support, the state of Israel asserted its claims without compromise. This

---

Like every ideology, Zionism hardened into a nonnegotiable cause that to many observers was no longer interested in or informed by the political facts on the ground.

---

included problematic implications for interaction
with the Palestinian population, which makes its own
claims and will not finally go away. One can argue that
the current ideology of Zionism is of a piece with that
ancient conquest of the "city of David," so that old
memories from the tradition have been readily coopted
as claims for the modern state of Israel. Clearly such a
preempting of tradition for such ideological purposes
indicates that Zionism does not equate with Judaism.

One can argue that the current ideology
of Zionism is of a piece with that ancient
conquest of the "city of David," so that
old memories from the tradition have been
readily coopted as claims for the
modern state of Israel.

MULTIPLE INTERPRETATIONS

It is important to distinguish between Jewish Zionism
and Christian Zionism, even though they make common cause in their support for the state of Israel. Jewish Zionism is grounded in what is understood to be
the nonnegotiable status of Israel as God's chosen people and the land as Israel's land of promise. Christian
Zionism is more complex. It includes a general sense
of solidarity with Jews that is informed by the long
legacy of Christian anti-Semitism. Its more vigorous
form, however, is grounded in a theological dispensa-
tionalism that regards the state of Israel as an essential
prerequisite to the "return of the Messiah." Either way,
Christian Zionism tends to regard the claims of Jewish

Zionism as absolute and nonnegotiable, a regard that yields singular commitment to the perceived interests of the state of Israel.

The claims of Zionism are exceedingly complex in the political world where a modern nation-state must exist. Moreover, Zionism itself is not uniform. Within the Jewish community, in Israel and elsewhere, there are Zionists who insist that there be no negotiations with the Palestinians, but there are also Zionists who believe that even with the legitimate claims of the state of Israel there must be a realistic coming to terms with the Palestinian leadership. The matter is contested acutely, even though the present government of Israel has been committed to a hard noncompromising position that refuses to engage in any serious negotiation.

Of equal complexity is church opinion toward Zionism. As indicated above, Christian Zionism is also multivoiced but is in general agreed to a singular commitment to the well-being and security of the state of Israel without consideration of any contextual realities. In the so-called American evangelical community, there is a deep attachment to the state of Israel that provides reliable support for a blank check in U.S. policy toward Israel. That evangelical support, however, is grounded in a belief about God's timeline in which it is held that after a millennium Christ will rule even over Israel. This belief is not, however, monolithic. Particularly among younger evangelicals, there is a greater inclination to break with such one-dimensional support for the state of Israel and to pay more attention to the facts on the ground that do not easily yield to any ideology.

Among so-called liberal Christians, the matter is equally complex. There is a greater readiness among liberal Christians to challenge the absoluteness of Israel's military posture (as is indicated by the 2014 vote of the Presbyterian General Assembly to divest from U.S. corporations that facilitate and profit from Israeli occupation). But those same liberals are reluctant to go very far with such criticism so as not to be seen as "anti-Semitic." After years of working in the United States to combat anti-Semitism among U.S. Christians and establish solid Jewish-Christian relations, many liberals are unwilling to put at risk those relations for fear of losing hard-won relationships. Yet, there is a growing conviction that it is possible (and necessary) to be critical of Israeli policy without being labeled and dismissed as anti-Jewish or anti-Semitic. But the matter is deeply contested among liberals as well, and many advocates for Zionism are determined to allow no open space between anti-Semitism and any critique of Israel and to bring any critique of state policy in Israel under severe moral reproach.

In the current manifestation of Zionism, biblical symbols, images, and metaphors are remarkably supple and can be developed in many directions, permitting a great play of imagination. Thus, *Zion* is variously available for the celebration of a past heritage and for the anticipation of future well-being. The image can be carried toward a secure Jewish homeland but in another instance may voice the mission of the church.

CONCLUSION

When a supple symbol or metaphor is taken up for a cause and hardened into an ideology, the elasticity disappears, and singular claims are made through it that resist alternative imagination and that seek to disregard sociopolitical facts on the ground for the sake of the ideology in a way that is increasingly dangerous to world order. The reduction of Zion to Zionism as a hardnosed ideology brings with it the danger of reducing the claim of God's fidelity to God's people into a one-dimensional possibility. The capacity to critique such ideology is exceedingly difficult, but it is characteristically the ongoing work of responsible faith to make such a critique of any ideology that co-opts faith for a one-dimensional cause that is taken to be above criticism. Indeed, ancient prophetic assessments of the Jerusalem establishment were just such a critique against a belief system that had reduced faith to a self-serving ideology. Because every uncompromising ideology reduces faith to an idolatry, such critical work in faith continues to be important.

Q&A WITH WALTER BRUEGGEMANN

1. The conflict between Israel and the Palestinians has polarized many liberal Christians in the United States. What do you see as the reasons for their differences?

Current attitudes toward the Israeli-Palestinian conflict are indeed polarizing. My own judgment—which is not an objective, detached judgment—is that the conflict of attitudes is between an old settled position and a more recent read of the situation that takes into account new facts on the ground. That old settled position was grounded in the realities of anti-Semitism, the brutality of the Shoah, and the risky bold founding of the state of Israel. That posture has ensured a deep commitment to the state of Israel, a commitment that in many cases is reinforced by cherished friendships with Jews. This attitude tends to pay lip service to Palestinian suffering but regards that to be of lesser importance and urgency than the deep debt that is owed to Jews and thus to the security and prosperity of the state of Israel.

An alternative to that settled position that I judge to be well informed does not deny the claims from the past— the force of anti-Semitism, the brutality of the Shoah— or the continuing vulnerability of Jews. But it also takes into account the current reality of Israeli military capacity that has long since moved past the vulnerability of the beginning of a fragile state, and it takes seriously the brutalizing, uncompromising policy of Israel toward the Palestinian people and their political future.

A constant in the conflict is the question of the security of the state of Israel, a concern about which both sides agree. But adjudicating between the well-established, well-funded, pro-Israeli perspective and a more recently emergent awareness of Palestinian suffering and deprivation at the hands of Israel is no easy matter. It requires more than the repetition of old settled mantras. In my judgment, it is important for liberal Christians to think well beyond long-held commitments that have remained uncriticized and that must now face a serious reconsideration in light of current realties on the ground. The actual suffering of human bodies and the deprivations imposed by harsh force expose as inadequate old ideologies that have long seemed to be beyond question.

2. Many are confused about whether or not the Israel mentioned in the Bible and scattered throughout ancient hymns and worship is the nation of Israel today. Some promote changing language in songs and litanies to avoid mentioning the word Israel. What do you think?

The ambiguity of the term *Israel* makes this issue difficult. On the one hand, there is a huge difference between the ancient Israel of the biblical text and the contemporary state of Israel. While defenders of the state of Israel insist upon the identity of the two, many more-critical observers see that there is a defining difference between a covenant people and a state that relies on military power without reference to covenantal restraints. On the other hand, there is the confusion stirred by a propensity on the part of the church to regard itself as the "true Israel" and the heir to Israel's promises and status, as reflected in Christian scripture and hymns. Paul insisted that the early church was "the Israel of God" (Gal. 6:16), and the lyrical articulation of 1 Peter 2:9–10 clearly intends to preempt the claims of ancient Israel from Sinai for the church as the carrier of covenant. There is something deep at stake theologically for the church to claim that it is "the Israel of God" and so the heir of the covenant with God. I am inclined to think, given the current turmoil about the state of Israel and the always present supersessionism, that we will do well to avoid such usage in the church. That is not always easy, given traditional hymns. At a minimum, we are required to exercise an acute theological sensibility that acknowledges the term is freighted in many ways that the original witnesses and hymn writers could not have imagined. On such a critical subject, the use of careful and intentional language is imperative.

3. What are the main mistakes you think people make about modern-day Israel?

The current state of Israel is laden with complex interpretive possibilities that are sure to lead to mistaken judgments and passion. In my view, it is a mistake

- to assume an easy and complete identity between the ancient Israel of the Bible and the contemporary state of Israel;
- to assess the current political conflict using the simplistic categories of biblical faith;
- to assume that because of a biblical legacy, contemporary Israel is entitled to the land and the Palestinians are not;
- to connect the current state of Israel to some imagined messianic time line that results in unilateral support for Israel;
- to imagine that such unilateral support for the state of Israel can or will eventuate in peace with the Palestinians; and
- to permit theological categories to blind us to the facts on the ground that entail occupation, oppression, and suffering. It is equally a mistake to imagine that real threats to Israel can somehow be wished away by biblical promises.

4. What do you see as a solution to the Palestinian-Israeli situation?

On the one hand, a solution to the Israeli-Palestinian situation would be immense and complex. On the other hand, I have heard it said that all informed parties to the conflict know within a cubit of territory and a syllable of formulation what the settlement will eventually be. There is, in my judgment, no realistic hope for any two-state solution. For all of the pretense and obfuscation of Israel, it never intends to allow a viable Palestinian state, so two-state negotiations simply buy more time for the development and expansion of the state of Israel. It may be that the solution will be found in a one-state solution that insists upon well-protected human rights for Palestinians while the Israeli occupation is fully recognized. A settlement will require an even-handed engagement by the Great Powers (including the United States) as well as acts of greater courage and political will by the immediate parties to the conflict.

5. How should U.S. Christians be involved in promoting a solution?

In my judgment, Christians must be zealous, relentless advocates for human rights. This means exposing the violations of human rights by all parties and recognizing the imbalance of power that make Israel's violations of human rights all the more ignominious. Christians must be zealous advocates with the U.S. government to check unilateral support of Israel as a bottom-line assumption. Our longstanding commitment to the security of Israel must be coupled with protection of human rights for Palestinians, not one without the other.

The core commandment of Christian faith is love of neighbor. In the end, Israelis and Palestinians are finally neighbors and have long been neighbors. When ideology coupled with unrivaled power is preferred to sharing the neighborhood, the chance for neighborliness is forfeited. Christians must pay attention to the possibility for neighborliness and must refuse protection and support for neighborhood bullies. Christians must support political efforts to strengthen the hand of the "middle body" of political opinion among Israelis and Palestinians to overcome the dominance of extremists on both sides who seem to want war and victory rather than peace and justice. Christians must call for new thinking in the U.S. government and do some new thinking that no longer assumes the old judgments about the vulnerability of Israel. Prophetic faith is characteristically contemporary in its anticipation of the purpose of God; it insists on truth-telling that is attentive to bodily suffering, and it refuses ideological pretenses. It will tell the truth in the face of distortions that come with ideological passion and unrestrained power. When truthfulness about human suffering is honored, new possibilities of a just kind can and do emerge. Thus, being able to differentiate between old mantras and urgent truthfulness is a beginning point for faithful engagement in the real world.

GLOSSARY

BCE and CE. Abbreviations for "before the Common Era" and "the Common Era" that often are used in place of BC and AD ("before Christ" and "anno Domini"). They developed in the scholarly world of biblical study, where Jews and Christians work side by side. In that setting, and in our culture at large as it is now developing, Christian domination is not appropriate or accurate.

For most of the first three hundred years of the Christian movement, Christians were a very small minority who shared with the Jews the common belief in God and a refusal to bow before the Roman emperors or deities. Thus, Christians began by sharing; it was a common era. It was only in the fifteenth century that BC and

AD came into common use, and it is only in the West, and because of the economic and military domination of the West, that they are used. In many other parts of the world, different symbols are employed that are only secondarily adjusted to fit the calendar of the West.

Davidic line. This term refers to David's descendants, who are also known as the house of David.

eschatology. That which has to do with the final judgment or the end of time.

exile. In July 587 BCE, Babylonian soldiers broke through Jerusalem's walls, ending a starvation siege that had lasted well over a year. They burned the city and Solomon's temple and took its king and many other leaders to Babylon as captives, leaving others to fend for themselves in the destroyed land. Many surrounding countries disappeared altogether when similar disasters befell them. But Judah did not. Instead, during the time scholars most often call the Babylonian exile, religious leaders were inspired to revise parts of Scripture that had been passed down to them. This period also sparked the writing of entirely new Scriptures and the revising of ideas about God, creation, and history. Much of what is called the Hebrew Bible or the Old Testament was written, edited, and compiled during and after this national tragedy.

millennialism. The belief that Christ will reign on earth for a golden age of one thousand years prior to a time of final judgment and a future world.

oracle. A message from God delivered through a prophet.

Realpolitik. From German, meaning "practical politics." Rather than conducting policy based on theoretical or ethical concerns, this refers to doing so based on the way things actually are happening on the ground.

Shoah. A Hebrew word used to refer to the murder of European Jews during World War II. Also known as the Holocaust.

supersessionism. The belief that Christianity has superseded or replaced Judaism as God's chosen religion. This view sees Judaism as a preparation for Christianity.

Torah. The first five books of the Hebrew Bible, which Christians usually call the Old Testament. Often called the Pentateuch in English.

YHWH. These four Hebrew consonants spell the divine name. In Exodus 3, God tells Moses to announce to the Israelites living as slaves in Egypt that God will liberate them from Pharaoh. Moses asks what name he should use for God, and God says, "YHWH" (v. 14), often translated "I am who I am" and pronounced "Yahweh."

Zion. Originally this was an actual location in Jerusalem on the southeastern hill of the city that became David's capitol and later the site of Solomon's temple. Biblical writers and poets used the term in symbolic ways that do not distinguish between the city, the temple, the monarchy, and the political-military apparatus. Zion became the symbol for a place of well-being assured by God's attentive presence.

Study Guide

INTRODUCTION
TO THE
STUDY GUIDE

THIS BRIEF STUDY GUIDE MAY BE ADAPTED AND USED IN a variety of situations. It suggests four sessions of approximately an hour. If desired, a fifth session may be created discussing the Questions and Answers Chapter and discussing potential group responses. A basic structure is provided for each session and a number of discussion questions are offered. Opening and closing prayers are provided. Adapt it for your group.

Many people have passionate feelings about the conflict between Israelis and Palestinians. This study will not resolve that conflict, of course. It can, however, help Christians grapple with some of the religious arguments made by competing sides. As much as possible, steer the conversation toward clarifying the author's arguments about what the Bible does and does not say.

PREPARING TO STUDY

- Organize your group, and have participants purchase their own copy of *Chosen?* or buy copies in bulk for a discount through www .TheThoughtfulChristian.com.
- Agree on a time and place to meet. Commit to read what will be discussed before arriving to each session. This will improve conversation and avoid a few individuals having to teach others what they have read.
- Arrange the space so that everyone can easily see everyone else. Place chairs in a circle or around a table.
- The facilitator's role is not to be the expert but rather to ensure that everyone has a chance to speak and that respect is always practiced.
- Create a welcoming, comfortable environment. Take a few minutes to introduce newcomers and to get to know one another.
- Read through this study guide and choose questions from each session that are of most interest to your group. You do not need to discuss every single question. Feel free to adapt them for your use.
- Session 1 has the group review an adapted version of some guidelines for respectful dialogue. See if your church or denomination has guidelines and make copies to use.

TEACHING TIPS

Acknowledge that you are not the expert on this issue. Tell participants that questions may arise that need to be investigated between sessions, and agree to share that responsibility. This will take pressure off you and help you concentrate on leading the session. If a question arises that needs an answer, write it on the board and continue the conversation. At the end of the session, agree on who will find the answer before the next session.

Read the entire book and this study guide before leading the group. This will help you do several things:

- Recommend to others how to read through parts of the book that may seem difficult. Walter Brueggemann is a biblical scholar, and some of the writing may seem technical at times. Encourage people to keep reading, and make a note of parts they want to clarify in the session. Use the glossary to introduce words that may not be familiar.
- Notice your own reactions to the book, and consider how others may react.
- Determine if you want to gather other resources for use during the study, such as historical and modern-day maps of the region.

GUIDELINES FOR RESPECTFUL DIALOGUE

IT IS GOOD FOR PEOPLE WITH DIFFERENT OPINIONS TO gather and discuss issues such as the Israeli-Palestinian conflict. Many groups create their own guidelines or adopt covenants such as this one, which was developed by the Presbyterian General Assembly in 1992 and is slightly adapted here.[10]

In a spirit of trust and love, we promise we will:

1. Treat each other respectfully so as to build trust, believing that we all desire to be faithful to Jesus the Christ.

   a. We will keep our conversations and communications open for candid and forthright exchange.

b. We will not ask questions or make statements in a way that will intimidate or judge others.

2. Learn about various positions on the topic of disagreement.

3. State what we think we heard and ask for clarification before responding in an effort to be sure we understand each other.

4. Share our concerns directly with individuals or groups with whom we have disagreements in a spirit of love and respect in keeping with Jesus' teachings.

5. Focus on ideas and suggestions instead of questioning people's motives, intelligence, or integrity.

6. Share our personal experiences about the subject of disagreement so that others may more fully understand our concerns.

7. Indicate where we agree with those of other viewpoints as well as where we disagree.

8. Seek to stay in community with each other though the discussion may be vigorous and full of tension.

9. Include our disagreement in our prayers, not praying for the triumph of our viewpoints, but seeking God's grace to listen attentively, to speak clearly, and to remain open to the vision God holds for us all.

Session 1

INTRODUCTION and READING THE BIBLE AMID THE ISRAELI-PALESTINIAN CONFLICT

OPENING

Welcome and Introductions

Welcome participants, and take care of any regular announcements or housekeeping logistics.

Ask people to think of a brief (under a minute) explanation of what interests them about this topic and what they hope to get out of this study. Use the process of mutual invitation to give responses. Mutual invitation is a process where the leader answers the question at hand. When the leader is finished, she or he invites another person in the group by name to respond to the question. That person can either pass or answer the question. After passing or answering, that person

invites someone else by name to respond. Continue
this until everyone has had a chance to speak.

Prayer

Say this prayer or one of your choosing:

*Holy One, we gather to study and reflect on a topic that
quickly raises fear, anger, and frustration. Calm our
hearts, open our minds, guide our time together so that
we all might learn something we did not know, reflect on
something we had not thought, and listen to one another
with respect and love. Amen.*

Affirm Guidelines for Discussion

Have people turn to page 70 and review the guidelines for
discussion. Invite them to add or edit the statement if they
wish; however, everyone must agree to the final guidelines.

QUESTIONS FOR DISCUSSION

1. The biblical writers reflect two different under-
   standings of inclusion/exclusion. Those who
   collected the scrolls/books in the form we now
   have them included both viewpoints.
   a. What was Ezra's argument for excluding for-
      eign wives and maintaining a "holy seed"?
   b. What was Jesus' reason for including for-
      eigners and those considered unpure?
   c. What, if anything, is the common intent behind
      the biblical views of inclusion and exclusion?

2. Brueggemann says the issues of interpretation that result in inclusion and exclusion have a long history in the religious tradition. African slaves, Jews, women, and now lesbian, gay, bisexual, and transgendered (LGBT) persons have always been included after a process of arguing about exclusion and inclusion. He says that the inclusion/exclusion of Palestinians is now the life-and-death issue. How do you think the arguments regarding the welcome of Palestinians are similar or dissimilar to those of the other groups mentioned?

3. On page 9, Brueggemann quotes Martha Nussbaum, who says the real clash of civilizations is not between Westerners and Muslims but is within each person as we struggle between self-protective aggression and the ability to live with others.
   a. Do you agree? Why or why not?
   b. What do you consider to be legitimate fears of the other?

4. On pages 10–12, Brueggemann suggests six conclusions about reading the Bible. A brief summary of these conclusions follows. Do you agree with the author? What would you add or change?

Conclusions

- The Bible speaks with multiple voices, and we must avoid simplistic readings.
- Any straight-line connection between the biblical text and contemporary issues is an oversimplification and can easily mislead.
- A straight-line reading is usually propelled by an ideology that seeks justification.

- This simplistic type of reading the Bible, in contrast to a more responsible reading that recognizes historical distance and complexity between the biblical and modern realities, can easily be used to justify exclusion of the other.
- Whoever the other group is or has been—enslaved Africans, women, LGBT persons, Palestinians—they will not go away. Ultimately, room must be made for them.
- At their core, the Ten Commandments articulate what a viable society must contain: loving God and neighbor. Destroying our neighbor destroys us in the process.

5. Read the quote from Desmond Tutu on pages 13–14. How would the liberation of Palestine liberate Israel?

CLOSING

Response

Go around the group (perhaps using mutual invitation) and ask people to quickly say one new thought, reflection, or question they will take from this session and think about in the coming week.

Closing Prayer

God of all, remove boundaries that exclude and hurt, and replace our fear of the other with trust and compassion. Bring peace to all places that are torn apart by war and violence. Give us courage to be active participants in making peace real. Amen.

GOD'S CHOSEN PEOPLE

OPENING

Welcome and Introductions

Welcome participants and introduce any newcomers. Spend a few minutes inviting reflections from the last session. If any questions were investigated, invite the person who found the answer to report to the group.

Prayer

Say this prayer or one of your choosing:

Gracious God, how good it is to gather and study with one another. As we study in the safety and comfort of this place, we remember those living in fear in Palestine and Israel, and we pray for an end to violence, which is often done in your name. Open our hearts and minds during this time of study. Amen.

QUESTIONS FOR DISCUSSION

1. In the first section of this chapter, Brueggemann points out that the Old Testament portrays a God "smitten with Israel." Why is God so enamored?

2. How does the Bible suggest this chosen status may be conditional? See Exodus 19:6.

3. Brueggemann identifies three ways the theme of chosenness has been appropriated by other groups: Christians, the United States, and liberation theology's claim that the oppressed are chosen or favored by God. How has each adapted the theme of chosenness, and why do you think it is or is not right to do this? What, if anything, is the danger of doing so?

4. How do you feel about the claim that some are especially chosen by God? What does this mean for those not chosen?

5. Brueggemann points out that the biblical text includes another understanding that argues against any exclusionary claim by Israel. What do we do with two competing sets of texts?

6. How do you understand the idea that the chosen must choose beyond their chosenness? What might this mean in today's conflict between Israel and Palestine?

CLOSING

Response

Go around the group (perhaps using mutual invitation) and ask people to quickly say one new thought, reflection, or question they will take from this session and think about in the coming week.

Prayer

Heavenly Creator, however you have chosen, may all people strive to live in peace and serve their neighbors, whoever they may be. Amen.

HOLY LAND?

OPENING

Welcome and Introductions

Welcome participants and introduce any newcomers. Spend a few minutes inviting reflections from the last session. If any questions were investigated, let the person who found the answer report to the group.

Prayer

Eternal One, calm our thoughts, help us focus, lead our discussion as we seek to discern your desire for us and our world. Amen.

QUESTIONS FOR DISCUSSION

1. What was the Deuteronomic *if* regarding the gift of land?
2. Brueggemann points out that the Torah ends before Israel enters the land. He says that this requires us to read the tradition with a double vision. Why is that?
3. The book of Joshua admits that there were already people living in the promised land. It offers several narratives of how the Israelites took the land and controlled it.
   a. How is the modern conflict between Israel and the Palestinians similar to the earlier biblical account?
   b. How should Joshua's warning that reiterates the Deuteronomic *if* be interpreted today?
   c. How central and indispensable for Judaism's existence are the land and the land promise?
4. Why is it unwise to make any direct appeal from the ancient promises of land to the state of Israel?
5. The legitimizing of the modern state of Israel as fulfilling God's gift of the land rests on a certain biblical interpretation. If one is not a Jew or Christian, should this religious belief have political force? If so, what about other religions' attempts to force nonbelievers to adhere to their religious interpretations, such as Sharia law?

CLOSING

Response

Go around the group (perhaps using mutual invitation) and ask people to quickly say one new thought, reflection, or question they will take from this session and think about in the coming week.

Prayer

Everlasting Father and Mother of all, awaken your people to your vision of peace. May your justice flow like everflowing streams throughout all your holy creation. Amen.

ZIONISM AND ISRAEL and Q&A WITH WALTER BRUEGGEMANN

OPENING

Welcome and Introductions

Welcome participants and introduce any newcomers. Spend a few minutes inviting reflections from the last session. If any questions were investigated, let the person who found the answer report to the group.

Prayer

Holy Creator, thank you for this opportunity to gather and learn and discuss important matters in an atmosphere of respect. May our discussion result in actions that further your cause of peace. Amen.

QUESTIONS FOR DISCUSSION

1. What is Zion, and how is it described in the Bible?
2. How did the symbol of Zion inspire hope when Jerusalem was destroyed?
3. Read the first paragraph in the section titled "Modern Zionism." How is a Jewish understanding of Zionism different from a Christian one?
4. There are a growing number of Jews and Christians who support the existence of Israel but are critical of its policies. Are they endangering the security of Israel by their open criticism? How should they express themselves?
5. Read the final paragraph. Do you think Zionism is a dangerous ideology? Why or why not?
6. Review the Question and Answer section (if you will not be doing an additional session). Discuss reactions to the author's answers.

CLOSING

One Thing I'll Do

Going around the group, invite each person to name one thing he or she will do as a result of this book study.

Prayer

Pray the prayer of St. Francis of Assisi:

Lord, make me an instrument of your peace.
Where there is hatred, let me sow love;
where there is injury, pardon;

where there is doubt, faith;
where there is despair, hope;
where there is darkness, light;
where there is sadness, joy.
O Divine Master, grant that I may not so much seek to
be consoled as to console;
to be understood as to understand;
to be loved as to love.
For it is in giving that we receive;
it is in pardoning that we are pardoned;
and it is in dying that we are born to eternal life.

ADDITIONAL QUESTIONS

Based on "Q&A with Walter Brueggemann"

QUESTION 1

1. What would you add or change, if anything, to the author's answer to the question?
2. Given that anti-Semitism still exists, many are afraid to criticize the state of Israel and the U.S. government's support of Israel for fear of being denounced as racist. How can one both support Israel's right to exist and also criticize it for its human rights abuses?
3. How should U.S. Christians discuss this matter with their Jewish friends who support Israel?

QUESTION 2

1. When you read the name *Israel* or *Zion* in the Bible, a litany, or a hymn, do you think of the modern-day state of Israel? Do you agree that it is wrong to equate modern-day Israel with biblical Israel? Why or why not?
2. Some Arab Christians report being unable to sing hymns that have the word *Israel* or *Zion* in them given the persecution they have experienced from the Israeli government. What would you say to them? Should their perspective lead to changes in the language of hymns in U.S. churches? Why or why not?

QUESTION 3

1. Which, if any, of the mistakes people make about modern-day Israel do you make? Is one worse or better than another?
2. How do you understand the final point made by the author?

QUESTION 4

1. How would you reply to this question?
2. Do you agree with the author? Why or why not? If you need more information, how can you get it?

QUESTION 5

1. Which of the suggestions the author gives do you think is most important?
2. What can you do to promote peace in the region?

NOTES

1. Joseph Blenkinsopp, *Ezra-Nehemiah: A Commentary,* Old Testament Library (Philadelphia: Westminster Press, 1988), 176.

2. Martha C. Nussbaum, *The Clash Within: Democracy, Religious Violence, and India's Future* (Cambridge, MA: Belknap Press, 2009), 15.

3. Ibid., 337.

4. Walter Harrelson, *The Ten Commandments and Human Rights* (Philadelphia: Fortress Press, 1980) , 186–88.

5. Ibid., 196–98.

6. Desmund Tutu, "My Plea to the People of Israel: Liberate Yourselves by Liberating Palestine," *Haaretz*, August 14, 2014, www.haaretz.com/opinion/1.610687.

7. Vladimir Putin, "A Plea for Caution from Russia," *New York Times,* September 12, 2013.

8. Todd Gitlin and Liel Leibovitz, *Chosen Peoples: America, Israel, and the Ordeals of Divine Election* (New York: Simon & Schuster, 2010), 190–91.

9. Martin Buber, *On the Bible: Eighteen Studies* (Syracuse, NY: Syracuse University Press, 2000), 29.

10. Guidelines for Respectful Dialogue adopted by Presbyterian General Assembly in 1992.

CPSIA information can be obtained
at www.ICGtesting.com
Printed in the USA
FFOW02n1814291115
19015FF